Scenes from the
Beach

by George Thatcher

QUAIL RIDGE PRESS
Brandon, Mississippi

Library of Congress Cataloging-in-Publication Data

Thatcher, George 1922-
    Scenes from the beach / by George Thatcher.
        p. cm.
    Includes bibliographical references.
    ISBN 1-893062-52-X
    1. Nature. 2. Beaches. 3. Seasons. I. Title.
QH81.T3394 2003
508.314′6—dc22   2003061129

Cover photo by Dr. Donald Bradburn.
Design by Cynthia Clark.

Manufactured in the United States of America.

 QUAIL RIDGE PRESS
P. O. Box 123 • Brandon, Mississippi 39043
Phone 1-601-825-2063 or 1-800-343-1583
Email: info@quailridge.com • Website: www.quailridge.com

To Marie Harris,
my talented editor,
the editorial director of
The Sun Herald,
who makes silk purses out
of sow's ears.

Acknowledgments

This is a successor to my earlier books, *Beach Walks* and *Beach Walks II*, published by Quail Ridge Press. All three books contain selections of daily columns published originally in *The Sun Herald*, the Knight Ridder newspaper serving South Mississippi. Both earlier books sold out.

I am very grateful to readers of both the newspaper column and the books. It is they who have made the column and the books successful.

Thanks go to Ricky Mathews, publisher of *The Sun Herald*, and to Stan Tiner, executive editor. Especially do I appreciate the talents of Marie Harris, the opinion page editor (to whom this book is dedicated). It is Marie who, for five years, has edited my scribblings, matching them with superb artwork.

I thank Gwen and Barney McKee, principals of Quail Ridge Press, for their faith in me, an unknown writer, and for their courage in publishing the first book. The people at Quail Ridge are an effective team, publishing quality books in Brandon, Mississippi. I am sincerely grateful to Sheila Williams, Cyndi Clark, Annette Goode, and all the other members of the Quail Ridge family.

Dr. Donald Bradburn, eminent pathologist and gifted nature photographer, resides in New Orleans and Ocean Springs, Mississippi. His masterful, beach photograph appears on the front cover. For his photograph and for his friendship I am most grateful.

The Mississippi Library Commission and the Library of Congress recorded my earlier books on audio tapes for the blind. I thank them for making the books available nationally to an appreciative audience.

Gratitude, too, goes to my beach friends—the gulls, terns, skimmers, pelicans, herons, sanderlings, cormorants, hermit crabs, barnacles, wildflowers, and all the others who are remembered fondly. What a wonderful cast!

George Thatcher
September 2003

Introduction

George Thatcher is the unofficial poet laureate of Coastal Mississippi. His daily dispatches in *The Sun Herald* provide witness to the incredible life and beauty on these tranquil shores. During his six years as the newspaper's essayist, he has drawn a wide following. Within his observations, his readers have discovered a brief respite from the tempest of news filled with crime, scandal and terrorism. His eye for detail allows all of us to see miracles in the mundane, small scenes observed beneath the microscope of a writer's lens, then painted in spare and eloquent prose. George's walks on the beach are retold through his many roles in life: historian, environmentalist and grandfather. The result is a treat for his readers who may have gone too long without the joy of sand between their toes. George takes us on a journey that enriches our souls and rejuvenates our sense of place.

—*Stan Tiner*
Vice President and Executive Editor of The Sun Herald,
a Knight Ridder newspaper covering South Mississippi

Author's Note:

I invite you to come with me on beach walks. Vicariously you will watch the shorebirds, feel the white sand underfoot, sense the sea wind, view the horizon, see a barrier island in the distance, dream of other days, and experience the peace and solitude of the moment.

People read books in different ways. I hope that you will read these pages sparingly—one or two at a time, surely not more than a few pages at a sitting. After reading a page, continue the walk mentally at your own pace; allow your mind to see more than the words convey. There is no continuity of subjects from one page to the next. Each page is a separate walk on a different day. Therefore, help retain a sense of time and the passage of days by limiting the number of pages you read.

G. T.

The Beach in

Autumn

"*Everything has the right to be left alone, even rocks and trees.*" *The words uttered by a former fishing boat captain have a measure of wisdom. Liberty, whether among people or beach creatures, is a priceless possession. Roosting quietly by the seawall this morning, a flock of gulls deserves its peace. The tall oaks, gracefully lining the beach road, have a right to be left undisturbed, as do sanderlings, at water's edge.*

Quoted by John Hay, *In the Company of Light;* Beacon Press, Boston (1998).

*E*mily Dickinson called the bird, a "winged beggar" and "beggar from the sky." Today a lone laughing gull hovers above a beach walker, begging to be tossed a bit of bread. A "plea for charity," the poet termed it. "Could I such a plea withstand?" she asked. Then giving the bird a crumb, she looked for some sign of gratitude from her "winged beggar." Given no bread, the gull flies away down the beach continuing its quest.

The Complete Poems of Emily Dickinson; Little Brown and Company, Boston (1960).

*S*unflowers blooming on the sand dunes attract butterflies which visit each blossom briefly, extracting a potion of nectar. The pretty yellow flowers appear to follow the sun's orbit, seeking either its warmth or light, perhaps both. William Blake described the sunflower as "weary of time," counting the steps of the sun. But looking to the western horizon this afternoon, the nimble blooms will expectantly face tomorrow's rising sun.

"Ah! Sun-Flower" by William Blake (1757-1826).

*T*he billowy, white clouds overhead now float to the north, guided by a mild south wind. Soon they disappear from sight to be observed by sky-watchers in the northerly counties. From the south other clouds drift into view. There continues a procession, one phalanx after another, all marching across the sky, their shadows on earth chasing their passage precisely. Watching the parade of clouds becomes a pleasant pastime.

Several days ago a piece of driftwood came ashore, waterlogged and heavy. It had been riddled with holes, the work of teredos, shipworms, sometimes called "termites of the sea." Now the wood is dry, bleached by the sun and as light as balsa.

Crumbling to the touch, the driftwood reveals a labyrinth of tunnels. The marine creatures are no longer there. In their place are small insects, occupying some of the teredo burrows.

$\mathcal{T}$he majesty of night is not often considered, but it has dramatic effect on beach creatures. It is a time of rest and quiet for most shorebirds, as  *it is, too, for other creatures. A time of dormancy for fish, night is virtually supreme until sunrise. City lights here weaken night's dominion, but darkness reigns farther to the south on the offshore islands. There the absence of light is challenged only by stars and a wan, veiled moon.*

*O*n the parched, bone-dry sand dune, a slender, green blade has appeared, a sprout of panic grass. Distantly located from its mother plant, the leaf emerges from a seed or perhaps from a long, underground root, snaking through arid sand. The leaf, cropping up here and surviving, brings the magic of new life to a desolate dune.

"I believe a leaf of grass is the journey-work of the stars," wrote Whitman.

Walt Whitman (1819-1892).

Sanderlings are easy to love! Some of the endearing little shorebirds remain on our beach all through the year, yet they are unlimited migrants, flying from the Arctic to the far reaches of both hemispheres. Truly global, they frequent beaches here as well as those in Europe, Africa and Asia. The whitest of sandpipers, sanderlings are the color of bleached sand. In flight, their flashing wing stripes are pleasing to watch.

Washed onto the beach this morning and now lying at water's edge is the upper valve of a scallop shell, riddled with holes. The shell tells the story of a hapless scallop attacked by hungry oyster drills, an example of the food chain at work. The scallop, like all biotic creatures, lived in an "eat or be eaten" environment. A fact not always grasped in civilized communities, the pierced shell tells us that the sea is still a primal jungle.

After an afternoon shower, a rainbow appears in the sky, its colors a striking contrast  *to the gray clouds. Today only four colors are visible, but scientists say that seven shades are always present. Add the missing colors? "To gild refined gold, to paint the lily, to throw perfume on the violet . . . add another hue unto the rainbow . . ." all are wasteful excess, wrote Shakespeare. So it is that a four-tinted rainbow arches the sky.*

King John, Act IV, scene ii, lines 11-16; *Asimov's Guide to Shakespeare;* Wings Books, New York (1970).

There is great restlessness among the shorebirds now. It is time for their autumn migration. Huge numbers of black skimmers in large flocks lift themselves from a roost on the sand beach, flying seaward in perfect unity, wheeling back again to the roost. The flight is repeated time and again. Although some skimmers will remain here all year, many will soon fly away to some southerly beach in Mexico or South America.

A night's rain has flattened yesterday's waves, becalming the surface.

   Today there are gentle swells, welling up on the beach then rushing back. It is as if the sea were breathing, inhaling and exhaling, a living thing. Our oneness with the sea may be explained in that 90 percent of our very blood is salt water, as is 60 percent of the body's weight. A taste of the sea's briny moisture to our lips tells us of an ageless kinship to the oceans.

Prayer Notes to a Friend by Edward Hays; Forest of Peace Publishing; Leavenworth, Kansas (2002).

A sure sign that autumn migration has begun in earnest is the appearance of a handsome marbled godwit at water's edge. The large, brown shorebird may have nested in the Canadian plains this summer and will winter in northern South America. Its bill, nearly five inches long, allows it to probe deep into wet sand for mollusks and worms. As walkers approach, the godwit sounds a shrill alarm, "whit . . . whit," and flies away.

*O*n stormy days like this one, frigate birds fly from their natural habitat on the barrier islands to the mainland. They are seen soaring high above the shoreline, effortlessly moving with the wind, their wide wings outstretched. Admired by countless people, the magnificent frigate bird is featured on at least 24 postage stamps issued by Grenada, Montserrat, Mexico, Colombia, Ecuador, Brazil and several other countries.

*A*mong the innocent pleasures of autumn is enjoying the simple dayflower, whose three petals have a striking deep blue color. A member of the spiderwort family, the plant blooms from April to November. So beautiful is the wildflower that some nurseries now cultivate dayflowers for sale. The blossoms, seen near the sand dune this morning, last only one day. Because their life span is so brief, their fleeting beauty must be enjoyed quickly.

*W*hen there is a tropical storm in the Gulf of Mexico, shorebirds sense the impending wind and waves. Although the disturbance is far away, huge flocks of gulls, skimmers, and terns gather on the beach; only a very few are airborne. Whether the birds detect a drop in barometric pressure is anybody's guess. Nevertheless, they somehow know that a storm is approaching, as they seek safety by flocking together.

The barrier island seen today on a misty horizon was called "Isle Aux Chats" by French explorers. On a 1732 map, only three decades after its discovery, the island is accurately drawn even to the shallow, sandy shoals surrounding it. What simple, but descriptive, names the explorers gave the islands—Ship Island, Round Island, Horn Island, Deer Island, Small Wood Island—all enduring three centuries are found on today's maps.

𝒜nother lovely gift of autumn's bird migration is a greater yellowlegs, which appeared on the beach this morning following an unexpected rain. The large sandpiper does in fact have long, yellow legs and a bill nearly three inches long. Soon it will leave for a winter home in South America, but for a while we will watch it gracefully feeding on the sand flats and hearing its lyrical, multi-noted call, "few, few, few, few, few, few."

*I*f only we could hear things talk, as Alice did in Wonderland! A whiting urged the snail to hurry to escape a porpoise; oysters and lobsters communicated too. Of course, things do speak, but we don't understand them. Gulls chatter in their flocks; skimmers bark messages; gales whistle through sails; waves whisper to the shore. Perhaps even little beach morning glories chat merrily as their blossoms open before sunrise.

Alice's Adventures in Wonderland; Through the Looking Glass, by Lewis Carroll (1832-1898).

The he herring gull was much admired by
Henry David Thoreau who called it "the
great gull" because of its size. In 1852, he
wrote in his journal that three of them
soared, wheeled, and circled "deliberately and
heavily yet gracefully." He also praised their
flight as capricious and undirected.
Thoreau's observations some 150 years ago
heighten esteem for a gull found daily on our
beach which is indeed a master of flight.

Henry David Thoreau (1817-1862).

The abundance of life in diverse forms at the shore is cause for wonder. Not only are there living things which we see—birds, fish, crabs, flowers and the like—there exist untold universes of microscopic beings. Rachel Carson, thinking about "the teeming life of the shore," wrote, "we have an uneasy sense . . . of some universal truth that lies just beyond our grasp," the mystery of procreation, the begetting and spawning.

The Edge of the Sea by Rachel Carson; New American Library, New York (1971).

This is the feast day of Saint Francis, that holy man who lived some 900 years ago. His love of nature and all its creatures has been celebrated by every generation. If he accompanied us on today's walk, what a companion he would be! He would address "our brother the sun, sister water, brother wind, sister moon, and our mother the earth." Francis would talk to the shorebirds and praise nature "who delights us with flowers."

"The Canticle of The Creatures" by Saint Francis of Assisi.

*A*merican Indians called this season the "time of falling leaves." And so it is. Tree foliage so green all summer is now browning, displaying occasional color. Longer hours of darkness deter the making of chlorophyll, the green pigment in plants. Soon dry leaves, bereft of life, will fall to the ground to be blown by autumn winds. Yeats wrote about the "lamentation of the leaves." Now trees will husband sap for springtime resurgence.

"The Sorrow of Love" by William Butler Yeats (1865-1939).

*B*each morning glories, white blossoms with delicate yellow centers, grow in profusion this morning by the fishing pier. "Breakfast enjoyed in the fine company of morning glories," wrote Basho, the Japanese poet on a day in the 17th Century. Another time he called upon his readers, "Come out to view the truth of flowers blooming in poverty." And so it is today, the splendid beauty of morning glory blossoms in arid sand.

The Sound of Water, translated by Sam Hamill; Shambhala, Boston & London (2000).

There are areas along the shoreline where small pebbles, bits of crushed seashells, and wood splinters accumulate, products of tide and current. Here today at these favored gathering spots are ruddy turnstones. Brilliantly colored little birds, cousins of plovers, they are busily overturning pebbles and shells with their bills in search of food. Their orange legs, black bibs, harlequin faces give them a striking appearance.

$\mathcal{I}$t is noon, and the shorebirds take a siesta, nap time. Occurring precisely at noon, low tide has caused wet sandbars to surface. In a few places exposed flats extend far out to sea. It is on the sandbars and flats that hundreds of birds gather. Gulls, skimmers, terns, pelicans, plovers, and others rest silently in warm sunlight. Some tuck their heads beneath a wing; some stand on one foot. As Eliot wrote, it is "the noon's repose."

T. S. Eliot: The Complete Poems and Plays; Harcourt, Brace & World, Inc., New York (1971).

Autumn witnesses the migration of shorebirds from nesting areas in some northern tundra to winter feeding venues to the south. Many migrating flights pass over this shore, some in unseen ghostly night passages. Even caged birds, it is said, attempt to flutter southward in autumn. Flights of plovers beginning in British Columbia may end in Argentina. The nomads are watched here each year much the same as they were by Aristotle in his time.

Morning Swells

Calm autumn sea breathes;
birds afloat, rise and fall on
softly rising swells.

The dune and the surrounding sand are marked by numbers of footprints today. A great blue heron left large, three-toed prints as it strode from the dune to the shoreline. Others were left by little fiddler crabs and ants, scurrying from one hole to another. A few different animal tracks are perhaps those of mice and nutria. This barren-looking mound of sand is host to many living creatures, some seen, others unseen.

The unity of art and nature was an objective that Cezanne and Walter Anderson shared. Anderson once inscribed "L 'hommage' a Cezanne" as a title for a watercolor. In his Horn Island logs, he describes the sea as "Cezanne blue." One thinks of the artist watching a skimmer slicing a calm, blue sea with its mandible as the sun sets. Indeed it was the skimmer for whom the Andersons named their business, Shearwater Pottery.

"The Voluptuous Return;" Copyright held by the family of Walter Inglis Anderson (1999).

Held in the hand, seeds from the top of tall dune grass are small, plain-looking snippets. It is difficult to understand that these tiny grains, appearing dead and meaningless, embody life. Are the tiny kernels pulsating even now with the planet's energy? Seeds often retain their life-renewing power for years before bursting forth in a reincarnation of the parent plant. Then in time other seeds appear in a mystical, eternal cycle.

*G*rowing in a hidden margin near a dune is a scrubby-looking, low-profile plant, all but devoid of leaves. Yet the barren, little bush has produced a perfectly formed, white bloom, beautiful beyond words. One day Jesus used wildflowers as an example in teaching his disciples. He said, ". . . not even Solomon in all his splendor was dressed like one of them . . ." And so it is that from a skinny, pinched bush, today elegance emerges.

Saint Luke 12:27.

$\mathcal{M}$ajestically, a line of 30-odd white pelicans at an elevation of about a hundred feet flies eastward. The huge birds, some with a wing span of nearly nine feet, are autumn and spring migrants, but a few may spend the winter here. Now the formation breaks, as the pelicans descend to the water, landing a few hundred feet away. There they float, a large flotilla, handsomely presenting their silhouettes, riding high in gentle waves.

*A*t sunset there is a huge congregation of shorebirds, more than three hundred, gathered close together just west of the fishing pier. Mostly gulls, the flock also includes skimmers, plovers, willets, peeps, terns, and two pelicans. All facing the setting sun, the birds are serenely still. One beach walker calls it their vesper hour, a time of peace when they silently contemplate day's end, the coming of night, and tomorrow's dawn.

*Daylight comes slowly as the sun rises.
A new day begins, not only for shorebirds,
but for all creation. It is a re-awakening,
a quickening to the pulse and tempo of a
turning planet. Moths, bats and owls retire.*

*Dune flowers
face eastward.
Insects emerge.
Fish swim faster.
Whitman called
it "the splendid
silent sun." The
coming of light*

*stirs and warms the earth for all its crea-
tures, as it has every day since the
world began.*

"Give Me the Splendid Silent Sun" by Walt Whitman.

A skiff moves along briskly a few hundred yards offshore. Powered by an outboard motor, it has a lone occupant seated astern, operating the engine. Years ago, the scene was different. One day Boris Pasternak rested his oars, feeling "the boat sway in my drowsy breast . . ." "Embrace the boundless skies . . ." he urged, "spend nights with nightingales and sighs!" Surely oars spawned more poetry than do outboard engines.

"Resting Oars" by Boris Pasternak; *Poems,* translated by Eugene M. Kayden; University of Michigan Press, Ann Arbor (1959).

The beach during daylight hours differs from the beach in darkness. During the day shorebirds are active, flying and feeding, but at night they roost silently near the seawall. An exception is the black skimmer, fishing all night, its harsh barking heard offshore. In darkness other creatures move about. Little sand crabs crawl, as do small dune animals whose tracks, leading to water's edge and returning, are found next day.

*A*n unexpected visit by two house finches is an agreeable way to begin a day. What blissful breakfast companions they are! Basho wrote about breakfast "enjoyed in the fine company of morning glories," but the little red finches are good company too. "Surprised by joy," Wordsworth wrote, and so we are today by the little birds' unforeseen beauty. Rare visitors here a few short years ago, house finches are now seen more frequently.

The Sound of Water, translated by Sam Hamill; Shambhala, Boston & London (2000).
"Surprised by Joy" by William Wordsworth.

The sea wears different faces. At dawn today, it was docile, calm with barely a ripple to be seen. At noon there were wavelets, a result of a mild breeze from the south. Now at day's end there are small whitecaps. The sea has displayed three varying faces in the span of a few hours. Melville reminds us that however peaceful the sea appears at the moment, the heart of a fierce animal pants below its surface.

Herman Melville (1819-1891).

If they were given intelligence tests, the herring gull and the fish crow would outscore other shorebirds. See them now, standing at water's edge a few feet apart, one seemingly unaware of the other. The slighting term "bird brain" is a misnomer when describing fish crows and herring gulls, because their thought processes rank them among the more intelligent birds. Alert avian brains help birds survive in hostile surroundings.

An immature heron in its first season lies dead on the beach. Visiting these shores frequently, death is no stranger to beach creatures. Why the heron perished is anyone's guess, but birds of the species are known to have lived for about seven years. Dying young is not limited to birds. How tragic in human life for Keats to have died at age 26 and Shelley at 30. Whether heron or poet, an early death is lamented.

John Keats (1795-1821).
Percy Bysshe Shelley (1792-1822).

Three mullet fishermen, throw nets in hand, wade on the sand flats at first light this morning. As did man far earlier than any extant record, beyond humanity's collective memory, they pursue their quest in a scene perhaps not unfamiliar to Homer. Although the intended quarry is mullet, their nets may ensnare speckled trout, a croaker or two, white trout, and maybe, if they are lucky today, a large flounder.

The wrack line, that beach contour
attained by high tide, is a repository of sea
treasures. Shells, fish skeletons, seaweed,
driftwood, torn nets, fishing lures, ropes,
bottles, plastic containers—all and more
are found along a wrack line. Sometimes
artfully shaped cypress knees, branches
which can be made into walking canes, life
preserver cushions, even large tree trunks are
found. Wrack lines are a beachcomber's
paradise.

*S*horebirds peacefully resting on a sandbar suddenly become agitated when an osprey flies high above them. The raptor, the birds think, poses an impending threat. But is it real fear or inherited instinct implanted eons ago by the birds' ancestors, "Flee when an osprey appears!" one wonders? Shorebirds always fly away from moving shadows, perhaps a collective memory of the umbra of raptors' wings in long ago Paleozoic times.

*B*efore daylight, thick fog descended on the beach, blanketing vision. With visibility limited to short distances, shorebirds were grounded in flocks near the seawall. The fog brought with it enveloping silence, even muting the lapping sound of the sea. Usually warm sunshine ends the haze, but today at noon the shoreline is still enshrouded. Like T. S. Eliot's woodthrush, a lone plover's plaintive cry is heard through the fog.

"Marina;" *T. S. Eliot: The Complete Poems and Plays;* Harcourt, Brace & World, New York (1962).

The day began with altocumulus clouds high in the sky, their fibrous plumes pleasant to watch. Some observers have likened clouds like these to sheep. Hoagy  *Carmichael called it a "buttermilk sky" and had all America singing his tune. Later gray nimbostratus clouds fill the sky. With the sun hidden, night comes early. A lone, large heron flies overhead, its low-pitched croaks the only sound heard in the near darkness.*

*F*locks of gulls
and skimmers, roosting on
exposed sandbars near shore are nervous
and flighty today. At the approach of beach
walkers, skimmers sound alarm first, then all
the birds fly away. Veteran walkers make an
effort to avoid roosting flocks. Expressing
the feeling, Thoreau made a journal entry in
1842, ". . . How is it that man always feels
like an interloper in nature, as if he had
intruded on the domains of bird and beast?"

Thoreau's Bird-Lore, edited by Francis H. Allen; Houghton Mifflin Company,
New York (1906).

*S*hrimp boats in the harbor are deserted, although one crew works on an engine. For the most part, the boats are local except one from Alabama. Some names are "Nothing Fancy," "Southern Cross," "Captain Phuong," "Tommye Bob." Several, however, have spiritual ones like, "Grace of God," "Santa Maria," "Lady of Lourdes," and "Sea Angel." The beauty of the seaworthy crafts is striking, as they rise and fall, straining their lines.

*T*here are worlds that exist beyond our knowing, things in nature so small that they cannot be seen with the eye alone. The use of a small glass reveals miniature wonders, everyday common objects that take on new life when magnified. A grain of sand becomes a glass boulder; a whelk egg case, a stylish tan necklace; sargasso weeds look like an undersea orchard; and a lowly fish scale appears to be iridescent slate.

*W*hen the tide recedes, leaving sand flats exposed, worms erect mounds, lighter in color than the ribbed sand. While they may be unpleasant to consider, they are not only food for shorebirds, but are also part of the beach's milieu. When removed far away from their former burrows, writes Rachel Carson, worms still rise and descend at the hours of tidal change at their aboriginal habitat. Such is their unexplained primal "memory" of tides.

The Sea Around Us by Rachel Carson; Golden Press, New York (1958).

*L*ittle hermit crabs in their "borrowed" shells bask on the beach today, confirming that they can live both in the sea and on dry land. Some move out of their shells to scavenge for detritus washed ashore, but quickly retreat into the chamber at a hint of danger. That classic fisherman, Izaak Walton, wrote in 1653 about a solitary crab occupying "a dead fish's shell, and, like a hermit, dwells there alone."

"The Compleat Angler" by Izaak Walton (1593-1683).

The Beach in

Winter

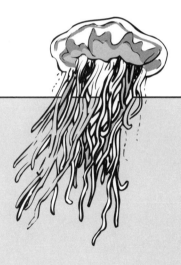

An artist—easel, canvas, brushes, palette, paint tubes, and chair all in place— surveys a seascape. He preserves this hour —this beach, its sand, the white-capped sea —capturing it on canvas to be remembered and savored. Like early man drawing in caves, like Seurat recalling a Sunday afternoon in a Paris park, or Van Gogh painting a starry night, the beach artist retains this afternoon on his canvas, redeeming fleeting memory.

There is something about the simple pastime of fishing that has broad appeal to all kinds of people—male and female, those of different races, rich and poor, educated and uneducated. It provides, Isaak Walton suggests, an escape from harsh reality. In "The Anglers Song," he intoned, "Life is . . . pain and sorrow, and short as a bubble; 'tis a hodge podge of business and money . . . but we will take no care, and Angle and Angle again."

"The Compleat Angler" by Isaak Walton (1593-1683).

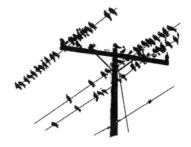

$\mathcal{A}$ cloud of starlings (little stars) descends on the beach, numbering more than a hundred. Wheeling out of the sky, they land in waves. Then about 20 of the birds perch on a utility line, displacing an annoyed kingfisher. In spring they will be a shining, glossy black color; but now in winter plumage, their buff hue with starry feathers identifies the species. Waddling, the birds walk along the shoreline at water's edge.

*O*n a sand dune a small
black spider has weaved a
complex web. Its silken
strands, stretching between
branches of a scrubby plant, shine in the
direct sunshine. Spiders are the most
patient of predators. The spinner of the
web expects an insect to snare itself soon.
Because there is little insect activity in the
winter, the spider may miss a meal or two.
But watchful and immobile, the spider waits
. . . waits . . . waits.

*L*ate on this December afternoon, a
few minutes before sunset, a brown pelican
occupies an offshore post. Alert, head down,
eyes searching the water below, the bird looks
for a final meal before nightfall. A target of
opportunity appears, a small fish swimming
near the post. Plummeting from its perch,
the pelican splashes into the water, grabbing
the fish in its bill. With slow wingbeats, it
flies away to roost on the beach.

The he three-note, wistful calls of a black-bellied plover carry over the sand. "Tooo-oooo-eeee," the lilt is repeated again and again. What is the message? There are no other shorebirds near. Does the little bird intone the notes for its own pure pleasure or is there an unseen mate nearby? About another bird Henry Van Dyke wrote, "An incantation so serene; so innocent, befits the scene: there's magic in that small bird's note."

Quoted in *Music of the Birds* by Land Elliott; Houghton Mifflin Company, Boston (1999).

*T*he densely green oak trees bordering the beach road would have delighted Oliver Wendell Holmes. It was he who praised the strange underground life of trees. The "great fluttering masses of leaves, stems, boughs, trunks," he wrote, are not the real thing, but only tails of trees. Consider for a moment the oaks' root systems, thrust deep into the earth, providing water and warmth, fountainheads of life for aboveground growth.

"Over the Teacups" by Oliver Wendell Holmes.

A dense fog envelops the coastland this morning. Reporting 100 percent humidity and poor visibility, the weather bureau has issued a marine advisory bulletin. So wet is the fog that it dampens both clothes and flesh. An oak tree near the beach road has extracted moisture from the fog. Drops of water fall from its branches as though it were actually raining. At its base, sparrows flit happily, welcoming the "raindrops."

*T*he dazzling color of this morning's sunrise has disappeared in the brightness of the day. But John Muir noted that "the grand show is eternal." It is always sunrise somewhere in the world, he pointed out. Dew never dries up completely; rain is always falling; fogs appear. "Eternal sunrise, eternal sunset, eternal dawn . . . on sea and continents and islands, each in its turn, as the round earth rolls . . .," he concluded.

John Muir: In His Own Words, edited by Peter Browning; Great West Books; Lafayette, Calif. (1988).

Watching loons on a winter afternoon is a pleasant pastime. Two of the elegant birds prefer the calm waters inside the breakwater, rather than the white-capped sea. Floating effortlessly, from time to time they dive for fish, remaining underwater more than half a minute. Although the water here is shallow, loons can dive 200 feet deep. Agile in water, the birds are ungainly on land, more often choosing to float.

$\mathcal{A}$ band of happy, little ruddy turnstones parades along the concrete fishing pier. Their orange legs, black bibs, light-colored underparts, slender bills, flashy black and white wing stripes in flight—all clearly identify the turnstones in their winter plumage. Shells, pebbles and minute sealife washed up on the pier attract the birds. It amazes one to think that these small, squat creatures are circumpolar in migration.

*I*n late afternoon fog first obscured the barrier island and then rolled ashore. From the shoreline, the  seawall, only 300 feet away, was no longer visible so dense was the heavy mist. Now at night the sound of a ship's foghorn, cautionary and plaintive, is heard repeatedly. Envision the ship's captain and the harbor pilot peering into the fog, consulting the radar screen and gyroscope, as the vessel inches down the channel.

$\mathcal{L}$OON

Stately loon floating
on glassy calm winter sea
dives with no ripples.

$\mathcal{F}$OG

Winter's misty fog
now drifting slowly shoreward
reaches the beach road.

*T*he beach this morning is in the hard grip of winter. Overnight temperatures dropped to near freezing, but the chill seems far below the thermometer reading. A stiff wind has driven the sea far out, exposing huge breadths of dry sand flats. How fitting that today is the winter solstice, the shortest day of the year. Since last June, each day has grown shorter, but now days will lengthen as the sun moves northward.

*W*hat is the
color of a sand
dune? The question
asked. The reply,
of course, is many
colors. Now in
mid-winter there is a
somber, grayish-brown, even the sand has
paled to gray. Once green, the panic grass,
and other small plants, having withdrawn
sap down into root systems, are crisply dry.
It is the color of death. But despite its
present guise, the dune is filled with life
ready to burst into color when spring comes.

*W*inter is a very special time to observe shorebirds. One author points out that birds are more relaxed now, like workmen on vacation, freed from arduous duties such as migration and nesting. Food here is plentiful even on cold days. It is a time when gulls and terns gather in huge, mixed flocks to roost on sandbars for hours at a time. It is a time too for us to celebrate the presence of our feathered, winter residents.

William R. Fontenot's text, *Birds of the Gulf Coast,* LSU Press, Baton Rouge (2001).

The sea this morning is calm as a sheltered mill pond, not a ripple to be seen. A small shell tossed into the water sends out little waves in an ever-larger circle from the point of impact. Cause and effect. A famous meteorologist, Edward Lorenz, theorized that the fluttering wings of a butterfly in China could cause a tornado in the U.S. One hopes that tossing a shell into the sea here will not result in a tsunami in Japan.

"The Butterfly Effect" by Edward Norton Lorenz.

Watching a pair of herons on a wintry afternoon becomes pure entertainment. For a while they stand stoically, unmoving, then one gambols away, running across the shallows, soon followed by the other. In observing herons (or any other creature), as John Leax points out, one does not seek

to invade their privacy, but rather to establish a neighborly familiarity, to greet the birds on the beach without "prying curiosity."

Out Walking by John Leax; Baker Books; Grand Rapids, Mich. (2000).

After three days of frigid temperatures, a small flock of black-bellied plovers rests near the seawall. Each one of the six birds stands on one leg, the other tucked away out of sight. They bask there in the early afternoon, like old men sitting on city park benches, enjoying the warm, winter sunshine. In a few months they will fly to northern nesting grounds in the Arctic tundra, returning here in autumn with young chicks.

In the dead of winter, there is a certain quiet which settles on the beach. For one thing, there are fewer people. There is less shorebird activity too, because the frenetic days of nesting and migration are past. Here now is eloquent silence. See the heron standing motionless in mute quietude. Basho observed in the 1600s that " . . . the air rings with silence." The day is soundless, a brief respite from a noisy world.

Matsuo Basho, Japanese poet, (1644-1694).

*T*wo fishermen on a commercial, small-craft harbor pier work on nets suspended above their boat this afternoon. Another tinkers at the vessel's diesel engine. The men prepare for shrimp season still months away. Long ago on another sea, James and John were mending their nets when Jesus called them. Earlier he had summoned two other fishermen, Peter and Andrew, to his ministry. Were they unlike the men at work here today?

The missing kingfisher has returned! After long absence, the little bird sits on the line which brings electricity to the fishing pier lights. Poised above the water, it watches intently for small fish to swim below its perch. Why does the bird bring happiness to a person's heart? Its forebears inspired poems by Gerard Manley Hopkins, Robert Lowell, William Henry Davies, and maybe others. Now the kingfisher flies away, trailing joy.

*A*mong human senses, the ability to touch is often minimized, but what wonderful messages it transmits to the brain. Feel grains in a handful of sand. Consider its origin, some faraway mountain. Hold a simple clam shell; count its growth lines; touch its smooth interior. Feel wavelets of seawater breaking on the beach, caressing your fingers. Simple pleasures, all are enjoyed by touch alone, not by sight, taste, smell or hearing.

*C*elebrate life! Extol all living organisms! Cherish and consecrate the diversity of life on earth. Consider humans, dune flowers, shorebirds, fish, insects, even sea worms, fungi and bacteria—all belong to life's five kingdoms. Albert Schweitzer held a reverence for life, not merely human life, but for all life. "For everything that lives is holy," wrote William Blake, "life delights in life."

The Five Kingdom System by professor R.H. Whitaker (1959).
"America: A Prophecy" by William Blake.

In a crack in the concrete seawall, a small, dark green plant has emerged. Five, delicate spatulate leaves reach laterally out of the crevice in all directions, seeking life-giving warmth from the sun on a cold, winter day. Of little value to anyone, the small weed survives in its own lifeless universe, surrounded by cheerless cement and drifting sand grains. Yet its greenness holds the promise of the coming of spring, still weeks away.

*L*ife, that spark of godhood, is a most precious gift, cherished by all creatures, including man. The will to survive is a strong emotion. Consider the large horseshoe crab, which came ashore in last night's high tide to lay eggs. Upended by waves, it lay helplessly stranded on its back for nearly fifteen hours. Yet the crab survived longer than most do. Returned to the water, it was motionless for a while before crawling away into the deep.

The shorebirds feeding at water's edge
today live at the fringe of civilization. Their
once-wild habitat, now encroached by people,
is reduced. Yet they maintain a sort of brave
isolation, as if a busy highway were not
nearby, ignoring beach walkers and city
noises. Just offshore, the barrier islands still
provide a remote, peaceful alternative.
Migrating soon, the birds will fly away to
more secluded domains for nesting.

The beach in winter offers a multitude of
blessings, but one cherished by shorebirds
is the absence of people. Unlike summer,
when the shoreline is crowded with scores of
sunbathers, the beach in winter is all but
deserted. Far to the east a runner plods
along. To the west, as far as eye can see,
there is no one. Miles away a small airplane
flies above the barrier island.
Here in sunlit quietude,
shorebirds feed silently
at water's edge.

*At noon the sun,
now at its zenith,
transforms the beach.
Life returns. Shorebirds
fly; a mullet jumps; a
dune flower blooms. We
recite Job's response, "Ask . . . the birds of
the air and they will tell you; or the plants
of the earth, and they will teach you; and
the fish of the sea will declare to you. Who
among all these does not know that the hand
of the Lord has done this? In his hand is
the life of every living thing."*

Job 12:7-10. Quoted in *Birds of the Gulf Coast* by Miller and Fontenot; LSU
Press, Baton Rouge (2001).

*W*inter is not the season for hermit crabs to visit our beach. Yet, nevertheless, here one is, laboriously dragging its shell along the beach, leaving telltale tracks in the damp sand. The crab knows its mission and destination, but both are a mystery to its observers. Picking up alluring shells, seldom does one think about the creatures which they once housed. What a pity, as we admire the industry of the little hermit crab today!

The little shell found on the beach this morning is barely an inch long, yet it is a thing of exquisite beauty. The geometry of the radiating, etched rays is stunning to the senses—far more complex than many of nature's other creations. Once the brittle shell housed a living creature, but now it is held in the palm and admired for its circular form, its ellipse, its finely sculptured shape, a gift from the sea to be treasured.

*W*ondering how he was perceived by the world, Sir Isaac Newton guessed that people considered him a boy picking up shells on the beach, ignoring a great gulf of truth, lying undiscovered. But, on occasion, what better thing to do? People should find time for shells, watching birds in flight, studying tracks in the sand, viewing the horizon, feeling a sea wind against the face, whiffing its fragrant essence—all simple pleasures.

Memoirs of Newton by Brewster.

A northeast wind, blowing at more than 10 knots, raking the beach all morning, discourages the shore birds from flying. Chilled by the low temperature, the birds gather now in small groups midway between the shoreline and the seawall. Rachel Carson once described a similar scene, ". . . The cries of the shore birds—twitter of sandpiper and bell note of the plover—were silenced, and only the wind's voice was heard."

Under the Sea Wind by Rachel Carson; Penguin Books, New York (1991).

In his Brothers Karamazov,
Dostoevsky stresses the value of love.
" . . . Love all of God's Creation, the whole
and every grain of sand of it. Love every leaf
. . . the animals, the plants, love everything
. . ." He wrote that if we love everything, we
will see the divine mystery in things. "Love
the whole world with an all-embracing love,"
he instructed. Shall we begin today with
this handful of wet sand?

Fyodor Dostoevsky (1821-81). Quoted in *Everything Belongs* by Richard Rohr;
Crossroad Publishing, New York (1999).

WINTER WIND

A winter wind blows
Gritty, sharp grains of white sand,
Stinging face and hands.

Selecting the tallest mast in the small craft harbor, a fish crow perches strategically high. The bird and all its ilk place their nests in the highest tree branches. In the 1700s, ships' captains installed casks near the masthead to provide the lookout protection from the weather. By 1818, "crow's nests" were universally used by all northern whalers. The fish crow peers downward, searching for detritus floating in the harbor.

The Oxford English Dictionary; Clarendon Press; Oxford (1989).

"*You will never enjoy the world aright til the sea itself floweth in your veins,*" wrote poet Thomas Traherne, "*til you are clothed with the heavens, and crowned with the stars . . .*" It means becoming one with the universe, heir to its treasures. The sea, stars, sky, wind, birds, sealife—all are gifts, free for the taking.

"*Perceive yourself to be the sole heir of the whole world,*" he reasoned, beneficiaries of God's largess.

Centuries of Meditations by Thomas Traherne (1636-1674).

*T*he larger crafts in the shrimp boat harbor—"the outside fleet"—will fish distant seas this summer, as far away as the Gulf of Campeche. Others,  the smaller vessels, termed the "inside fleet," will venture no farther than the coastal waters of the northern gulf. Both fleets lie somnolent now, their masts pointed skyward, lines sounding gentle chimes as they flap against metal in a soft wind, green nets suspended above decks.

Things seen and heard on today's beach walk: A family of six lesser scaups, small, blackish, floating ducks, all dive together as if on cue. A huge herring gull perches atop a piling, unmoving, staring seaward. Flying away at the approach of walkers, a kingfisher disappears into the fog. Distantly, in dense fog, a passing ship sounds its horn, warning all of its presence. Now the misty fog nears, enveloping the beach in its wetness.

The sea, docile for nearly a month, is white-capped with frothy waves coming ashore every six seconds. Small craft flags have been hoisted, warning of 25-knot winds and 4-foot waves near shore. Pieces of driftwood are already washing up where at high tide they will be left high and dry along a wrack line. Tomorrow, beachcombers will find the sea's gifts—cypress knees, shells, fishing gear, grasses, and other mundane, wondrous stuff.

In the north
sky tonight, there
are the Big Dipper
(Ursa Major), the North Star (Polaris), and
to the left Cassiopeia (The Queen).
Through the ages, the beauty of the stars
has been sung by seamen, poets, and
philosophers. Ptolemy remarked, ". . . when
I trace, at my pleasure, the winding to and
fro of the heavenly bodies, I no longer touch
earth with my feet; I stand in the presence
of Zeus, himself, and take my fill of
ambrosia . . ."

Ptolemy (100-178 A.D.). Quoted in *The Common Reader* (Winter 2001),
Pleasantville, N.Y.
www.earthsky.com (February 2001)

*E*nshrouded by fog this afternoon, the beach provides one a sense of solitude. Vision is limited to a distance of only a few feet; consequently, sounds become more noticeable. It is said that blind people depend on a heightened sense of hearing. The distant din of traffic, a faraway train whistle, wavelets coming ashore, black skimmers barking somewhere over water, a willet's frightened "keetee"—all are sounds of things unseen.

OAK LEAF

In winter's still hush
a lone, green, oak leaf flutters.
Others hold their breath.

CLOUDS

High above, clouds scud
across, February's sky
chased by the north wind.

The intensity of the sun is welcomed this cold February day, a gladly received blessing following days of dank, dense fog. Now high in the sky, the sun is brilliant, warming, and comforting. It creates on the sea different hues of blue, darker in the distance, lighter azures near the shoreline. In his hymn to the sun, Saint Francis sang, "Praise to thee, my Lord, for all thy creatures, above all Brother Sun."

"The Song of Brother Sun" by Saint Francis of Assisi (1181-1226).

In the darkness of a winter's night, clouds obscure both moon and stars, making it even blacker. ". . . Darkness reminds us of light . . . ," intoned T. S. Eliot. Think back to that time before the day of creation when there was no light at all. ". . . There was darkness over the deep . . . ," the author of Genesis recounts. But as night cloaks both sea and land tonight, its dismal gloom will end at sunrise in the light of another day.

"Choruses from 'The Rock,'" *T. S. Eliot: The Complete Poems and Plays;* Harcourt, Brace, and World, Inc., New York (1971).

The early morning sea is placid, becalmed on a windless day. So reflective is the surface that images of slow-moving, overhead clouds are mirrored. Very much like a looking glass, the sea reflects shorebirds as they fly above it. At intervals the surface is disturbed by the dive of a tern or by a fish jumping. The resulting ripples, concentric circles ever widening, finally dissipate, leaving the sea mirror-like once again.

Silhouetted against a setting sun, a double-crested cormorant is poised atop an offshore post. Its aesthetic, oriental beauty, framed by a crimson sky, is a work of art, worthy of being preserved on canvas by a skilled artist. The slender, curvaceous neck is statuesque. A camera could not record this moment of elegance. A lens would fail to capture the evening's quietude—a glass-like, windless sea; the peace and hush of day's end.

The coastal plain which extends from the sea northward can boast of hills, but certainly no mountains. Yet at sunset today a bank of clouds on the western horizon looks very much like a range of towering mountains. Silhouetting the dark blue clouds, an orange sun slips below the horizon. One can see the clouds' craggy peaks and rock-strewn valleys. If only briefly in one's imagination, this coastland has its own dream-like mountains.

*O*rkney Island poet, George Mackay Brown, wrote of a beachcomber's week. On Monday he found a boot and gave it back to the sea "to dance in." A timber spar on Tuesday, enough to make a chair. On Wednesday, whiskey which he drank, because "the shore was cold with mermaids and angels." On Thursday, only seaweed and bones, "wet feet and a loud cough." Sunday he sat and dreamed of heaven—"a sea chest with a thousand gold coins."

"Beachcomber" by George Mackay Brown (1921-96); *A New Treasury of Poetry;* Stewart, Tabori & Chang, New York (1990).

*O*n shore this afternoon the wind velocity reaches about 12 knots, but offshore (electronic weather buoys report on the Internet) a gale  gusts to more than 20 knots. It is very pleasant, Charles Darwin once observed, to see a squall from shore, and quite another thing to experience the same tempest at sea. Far out in the intracoastal canal, barges are pushed by a tug, whose deck hands, one guesses, would agree today with Darwin.

The scarred, pitted, and worn scallop shell picked up this morning would not interest a collector, but it is appealing to this beach walker. The beauty of its sculpture is still intact. Camouflaged, the top valve has protective coloring. In antiquity, scallop shells were cherished talismans for Christian pilgrims. Among others, Sir Walter Raleigh requested a "scallop-shell" for his pilgrimage in 1604.

"The Passionate Man's Pilgrimage" by Sir Walter Raleigh.

The Beach in Spring

*S*easons change. Winter ends,
spring begins. Gulls take on their breeding
colors. Wisteria blooms open on the vine
which entwines the live oak. Schools of
small fish come near shore. The seasons,
wrote James Thomson, "are but the varied
God, The rolling year is full of Thee . . . in
the pleasing Spring, Thy beauty walks . . .
And every sense and every heart is joy."
A bright springtime sun shines on a
sparkling sea this morning.

James Thomson (1700-1748). *Invisible Light, Poems About God,* edited by
Diana Culbertson; Columbia University Press (2000).

Winter stalks away, leaving in its absence cool mornings, blue skies, and a sense that life returns once again to a barren beach. There is a call to be alert to seemingly irrelevant changes in nature—an early wildflower bud, a warming sea, southerly breezes rather than north winds, a more radiant sun, lucent and longer days, the coming and going of migrant birds—all of which proclaim the advent of spring, the promise of summer.

*C*elebrating the first day of spring, black skimmers have returned. Although some of the species are permanent residents here, many skimmers winter as far away as Argentina. Two large flocks of more than 30 birds each fly eastward 20 or so feet above the surface of the sea. Later both groups return, flying to the west. Near the fishing pier, skimmers fly buoyantly, their mandibles slicing the calm water.

*T*here is sorrow at the death of a bird. A cormorant, flying and diving joyously yesterday, now lies lifeless. Serene in mortality, the fallen bird lies there, its long slender neck outstretched gracefully, its plumage black in contrast to the white sand, the spark of life gone forever. ". . . And if they are sad about how they must wither and die," Rilke conjectured, "perhaps it is our vocation to be their regret . . ."

"Sonnets to Orpheus," II,14: *The Selected Poetry of Rainer Maria Rilke;* Random House, New York (1982).

The family of beach creatures is roughly divided into two groups—those with spinal columns and those without. Invertebrates outnumber their bony cousins by hundreds of thousands. They include jelly- 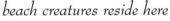 *fish, crabs, worms, sea urchins, clams, shrimp, and many more. Vertebrates are fish, birds, humans, and frogs. Regardless of their many differences, beach creatures reside here*

in community, all pulsating with God-given life.

Under cloudy skies, a southerly wind rose before daylight and is now at gale force. Line upon line, file upon file, battalions of waves form for battle:

WAVES
A cold spring wind sends
foaming waves marching shoreward.
Fresh troops attacking.

*O*f all shorebirds which grace this coastland, snowy egrets are surely the loveliest.
One bird book describes them as ". . . the
daintiest and most exquisite."
Now in breeding plumage, the
dazzling white feathers are
brilliant under the noon
sun. But it is their richly
gold-colored feet which
give the birds quick identity.
The three here today may be
migrating northward because they appear
larger than our local egrets.

The Audubon Society Encyclopedia of North American Birds by John K. Terres;
New York: Alfred A. Knopf (1980).

A pod of four dolphins swims by this afternoon. Celebrate their wildness! Unfettered and untamed, they move parallel to the beach, coming near shore to feed at high tide. See them swim near the surface, their fins frequently visible. They are wild, primeval creatures as free and feral as tigers in an immense forest. Gerald Manley Hopkins, phrased it nicely in 1881, "Let them be left, O let them be left, wildness and wet . . ."

"Inversnaid;" *The Oxford Authors: Gerard Manley Hopkins;* Oxford University Press, Oxford (1986).

*S*culpted by the sea in the shape of a dolphin's head, a large piece of driftwood has floated ashore. Of course, the sea is not a skilled sculptor and had no intention whatsoever of producing a work of  art. Yet the driftwood, floating in the sea, pounded by waves, scraped against abrasive sand bottoms, cut by shells, driven into pilings and concrete groins, has been transformed into artful sculpture.

*F*ollowing a busy weekend, there are myriad footprints in the sand: small imprints from children's bare feet, larger adult ones, and some shoe prints at water's edge left there by runners. On a different beach the author Macrina Wiederkehr touched such footprints and prayed for each owner in a silent blessing. It called to her

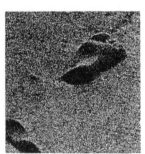

mind, she wrote, a Coleridge verse, "A stream of love burst upon my heart, and I blessed them unaware."

A Tree Full of Angels by Macrina Wiederkehr; Harper Collins, San Francisco (1990).
Samuel Taylor Coleridge (1772-1834).

*F*inding beauty in ordinary things may be a surprise to some, but for beach walkers it is a normal occurrence. The ethereal flight of our most numerous gulls, a faded bloom of a dune flower, lavender blossoms on wild wisteria vines, a billowy, white cloud passing overhead, the order of minnows swimming at water's edge, a mullet jumping—all are embraced in an appreciation of plain things, sometimes ignored by busy people.

*I*f any shorebird deserves the word "grace," surely it is the black skimmer. Flights of about six birds each wing eastward near shore where the water is calm, mandibles slicing the smooth surface. Soon they disappear from sight, only to return on westward courses a few minutes later. With  black wings and head, white underparts, bright red bills and legs, they fly with pure artistry, veering shoreward to land on the beach.

Awareness is a wonderful gift. On this pleasant afternoon, one is keenly cognizant of things—the white sand, the blue sea and sky, the cool breeze. The comb jellyfish at water's edge shares the gift too. It is aware of its existence, as are the gulls flying overhead. But what of the yellow flower on the sand dune, following the sun's orbit? Is it aware too? The bloom, one guesses, somehow merely senses the sun's presence.

MARCH FOG

A herring gull flies
into a March morning fog,
vanishing quickly

ife, a succession of days, was com-
pressed into one day by Doris Grumbach in
her book. A potted flower became her entire
garden. A meditation, a monastery. The
view of the sea from her window, the whole
world itself. But sometimes we live our days
unknowingly, sometimes allowing hours to
escape without notice, sometimes forgetting
that this one day, this hour, this very
moment is ours to savor to the fullest.

Life in a Day by Doris Grumbach; Boston: Beacon Press (1996).

*S*cores of laughing gulls are assembled
near the seawall in a large roosting flock.
In nesting plumage, the birds have strikingly
black hoods, gray wings, and white bodies.
Gulls have been on earth since the Eocene
epoch, about the time mammals arrived.
Through all the ages, God must have loved
them dearly, because there are so many
of them. Now they have lift-off, flying
seaward, soaring, wheeling, turning, and
then land again.

The thought of spending even a few minutes simply doing nothing is an alien experience for many of us. After all, the work ethic by which we live tells us to stay busy, to be productive. Yet there is much to be said for doing nothing, thinking of nothing. Merely sitting, yawning, maybe relaxing, but are there not birds to watch, shells to find? Pardon my sitting here on the seawall doing nothing for a while.

A harbinger of summer is a sulphur butterfly, fluttering in the early morning air. The first butterfly of the season brings with

it a promise of spring and other species of its ilk. "Butterflies are but flowers that blew away one sunny day . . . ," wrote George Sand in one of her more poetic sentences. The lone sulphur flies across an open field near the beach, stopping for a while at wild clover and dandelion flowers.

Quoted in *A Common Reader,* The Akadine Press, Inc., Pleasantville, N.Y. (January 2002).

The greening of the sand dunes has begun. The first evidence was the appearance of green among minute plants which grow at the feet of tall, brown panic grass stalks. If one looks carefully, he sees small blades of green growth emerging from the stalks themselves. The plants' sap, which  *had descended to the root systems last autumn, rises once again. Keats called it "the tender greening of April . . ."*

John Keats (1795-1821).

There is a pattern of white caps rolling ashore this afternoon. Driven by an 11-knot south-by-southeast wind, the waves break on the shore every six seconds then recede into the sea. Because this is the hour of high tide, each wave reaches farther up the beach. Pulled by the moon, powered by the wind, they invade the mainland for a while. When the tide ebbs, the waves will withdraw a bit, allowing the mainland to regain its shoreline once again.

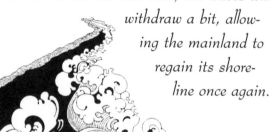

*A*pril is the month when millions of monarch butterflies leave the high Sierra Madre mountains in Mexico for arduous migration across the Gulf. After a fortnight's flight, they will reach our Coast, always a happy event for viewers. With wingspans of $3^1/2$ inches, monarchs may fly some 3,000 miles and by summer will occupy the hemisphere. On the Coast, they will take nectar from seaside goldenrod and other plants.

Handbook for Butterfly Watchers, by Robert Michael Pyle; New York: Houghton-Mifflin Company (1992).

$\mathcal{I}$t is late in the season for cormorants to be here. In most years by now they have migrated north, having flown above tempting Delta catfish farms to nest by remote Canadian lakes. Yet there sit five cormorants atop posts just offshore. One dries its spread wings; another plummets into the water after a fish. Milton once compared Satan to a cormorant. But now the birds look almost benign, very much a part of their milieu.

Paradise Lost, Part IV, by John Milton.

*S*pring brings with it renewed life—
a time of rebirth. A seed buried in cold, wet
autumn now bursts out of a cocoon of death.
Atop the dune, a small, solitary blade of
green grass appears, growing from grains of
damp sand. The new growth is the only
sign of life on the dune. The earth is
          "inhaling life from the universe,
             expanding, budding, straining
                to send forth . . ." a new
                generation, writes Shusako
                Endo.

Scandal by Shusako Endo; New York: Dodd, Mead & Co. (1988).

This morning's unusually high, spring tide left many moon jellyfish stranded far up on the beach. Much hardier than comb jellies, moons are burly enough to survive the trauma of being stranded. Beach walkers carefully place the moons (some 18 inches across) back into the water, where aided by a north wind they will float to safety in the open sea. As they lie in shallow water, their translucent bodies visibly pulsate with life.

*C*arl Sandburg told of a fish vendor who
sold his catch with joy, "terribly glad to be
selling fish, terribly glad that God made fish"
and glad too for customers. The poem
brings to mind our own local vendor who
slowly plied the streets in his ancient truck.
"The Oyster Man from Pass Christian,"
his voice boomed, "nice good ones, real fine
ones." The happy peddler, hawking his
wares here in the 1930s still lives in
memory.

"The Fish Crier" by Carl Sandburg; *The Complete Poems of Carl Sandburg;*
Harcourt Brace & Co., New York (1988).

*P*icking up a bleached white skeleton of a gafftop sail catfish, one holds a remarkable crucifix. Although it is merely the fish's bone structure, it is surely the figure of a person crucified—head erect, arms outstretched, wounded hands—clearly depicted. Why would Jesus sanction His likeness to appear in such an humble manner? Recall that it was He, once born in a manger, wearing swaddling clothes, who chose to die poor and naked.

The least terns have returned! A single bird was sighted yesterday; many more today. Celebrate their arrival, a joyous event! What a pleasure there is in watching them fly at 10 feet or so above the water, heads down, wings flapping to maintain stationary positions, then diving headfirst to take tiny minnows to their nests. It is there where the eggs will be laid, and there where the chicks will hatch by early summer.

*W*atching gulls fly this afternoon is a joy-filled pastime. Some are acrobatic and graceful, like ballerinas soaring, swooping, and gliding. How birds fly puzzled Leonardo da Vinci in his day, and also baffles scientists now. A bird is not an airplane, remarked one writer. A few birds fly despite aerodynamic laws, which maintain that they cannot possibly become airborne. Stationary now, a gull hovers. It is a miracle of avian flight.

"The Mystery of Flight" by Doug Stewart; *National Wildlife Magazine;* National Wildlife Federation (February/March 1996).

Today high tide still comes late in the day. Soon, however, it will be in morning hours, continuing that cycle through summer and early autumn. Humans rarely know when the tide changes, but shorebirds perceive it at once. In the 19th century, Audubon noted that brown pelicans were "the most watchful" of all shorebirds for tidal change. At the instant the tide begins to flow, pelicans are the first to become active, he observed.

"The Brown Pelican" by John James Audubon (1785-1851).

*W*hen high tide occurs in the morning calm, it is easier to spot dolphins than at other times. As a rule, dolphins come near shore with the tide, because it is then that fish—speckles, mullet, croakers and other— also approach the beach. A pod of three dolphins swims westward, parallel to the shoreline. The calm sea is broken by their fins as they surface to breathe time and again. On other days, dolphins may pass unseen.

When waves break against the beached driftwood log, a fine spray is sent into the air, blown landward by the south wind. Salty droplets from the spray strike the lips. If Emerson were here, he could tell us that a briny droplet is a microcosm of the entire universe, a diminutive representative of all Nature. *"The world globes itself in a drop of dew,"* and this very day is but a *"miniature eternity,"* he once wrote.

Journals of Ralph Waldo Emerson (1803-1882).

A meditation on a seashell: Picked up at water's edge, it is a simple, small scallop shell. Once it was a bivalve, housing a tiny animal in intertidal water. Now we admire the shell with its sculptured, radial rays, fan-like, a mottled brown. In the Middle Ages, pilgrims placed such shells on their hats as identification ("badges of St. James"). And Botticelli once painted Venus rising exquisitely from a scallop shell.

"The Birth of Venus" by Sandro Botticelli; Uffizi Gallery, Florence.

*I*n the hours before daylight, a waning, but brilliant moon rides high, flooding the sky with light. Having blown at gale levels all day, the wind has now ceased, and the sea's surface is broken only by gentle ripples. Off shore, black skimmers bark as they fish. William Blake wrote of such a night, "The moon like a flower, In Heaven's high bower, With silent delight, Sits and smiles on the night."

"Night" by William Blake (1757-1827).

$\mathcal{L}$arge tracks of a great blue heron are found today by the sand dune. Probably going there in search of fiddler crabs, the heron left a trail of footprints from water's edge at the site where it often stands in shallow water. There are other tracks as well near the dune—of gulls, plovers, those of a small animal and ants. Tracks are best observed when the sand is damp; otherwise, even a light wind erases footprints quickly.

*S*tanding at water's edge, a plover is
motionless, resting after a busy morning
of feeding. Is its tiny brain capable of
memory? Does it recall a winter range in
the pleasant grasslands of
Argentina or a cool summer
nest on a faraway tundra? Is
there a faint mental flashback of a
particularly fierce wind or the recollection of a
dreaded raptor attack? Is the plover aware
of yesterday's events or even those of earlier
this morning?

A shrimp boat moving southward in the channel today is in the proud tradition of fishing, a long history of man in pursuit of seafood. On this continent Norsemen angled a thousand years ago. And even earlier natives cast nets along these shores. There is a mystical bond which links the boat crew today, not only with North American fishermen, but also with all those others everywhere who have spread nets since the dawn of time.

"*It is a great art to saunter,*" wrote Henry David Thoreau in his journal. Beach walkers agree. Walking leisurely along the beach with no particular desti-  nation in mind, picking up a shell at random, looking at driftwood here and there, sensing the waves, the beach walker is on a lark, a furlough of sorts from the business of living. Although strolling is an art, there is also an art in simply sitting on the seawall, doing nothing.

The endless procession of horseshoe crabs continues this spring. An act of procreation, they come ashore, couple, bury their eggs in the sand, and return to deep water. The act is one of silence. They silently come from the sea, silently dig trenches for the eggs, then silently return to the deep. If only they could but speak for themselves, sharing with us the recalled cycles of life in all the epochs, yet even their silence speaks volumes.

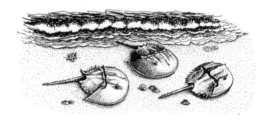

Several days ago clumps of sargassum,
the gulfweed, covered the shoreline.
Dry now, the growths retain their beauty.

GULFWEEDS
Gulfweeds float ashore,
brown bouquets, gifts from the sea,
obeying the wind.

*G*rowing prettily along the beach road,
a yellow sweet clover flower is among the
season's early bloomers. Its five petals,
spread open to sunshine while growing, close
abruptly when picked. Whether to pick a
wild flower is a difficult choice, even if the
picker will be the only human to see the
flower during its life span. Unseen by
others, its beauty is pleasing, far more
appealing to view alive than as withered
petals.

"The art of spending a day" occupied the mind of Henry David Thoreau as he wrote his journal in 1851. He noted that most men did not know how to spend a day properly, and decided to become nature's watchman rather than to merely "eat oysters," as he put it. "My profession," he vowed, ". . . is to find God in Nature— to know his lurking places . . ." Reason enough, one supposes, to walk the beach daily and to be its "watchman."

Wild Fruits by Henry David Thoreau; edited by Bradley P. Dean; W. W. Norton & Co., New York (2000).

A handsome osprey perches atop an offshore post, head bowed, its keen eyes scanning the water below for prey. Commonly called "fish hawk," the osprey is among the most regal of birds. For years, along with the brown pelican, it disappeared from this coastland. But now it has returned in its august, royal beauty, the kingly raptor, monarch of all our shorebirds. There it sits, imperiously waiting for a suitable fish to swim by.

*I*n past years the numbers of plovers and turnstones have declined in the late spring and summer, as the birds seek cooler climes. But there are still many of the little plovers on the beach. Orange legs set turnstones apart from other birds. Fossils of their early ancestors date from the Oligocene epoch of the tertiary period, 25 to 40 million years ago. Here they are today, totally unaware of their long tenancy on earth.

Gulls and Plovers by C. J. Barnard & D. B. A. Thompson; Columbia University Press, New York (1985).

*L*arge, shapely horse conch shells are not found here often. The one at water's edge today is pulled along by its current occupant, a striped hermit crab, leaving tracks on the wet sand. When the shell is picked up and examined, the hermit crab retreats into the farthest chambers. The poor creature must think that it is doomed, expecting to be eaten by a predator. Returned to the sand, it quickly disappears into a green sea.

Yesterday's high winds and heavy rains have taken their toll. At water's edge this morning are the bodies of two large birds, a brown pelican and a great blue heron. They lie near each other with wavelets breaking against them. In death, their inert, limp bodies lie in awkward positions, moved there by the waves. Their demise defines the fragility of beach creatures. A simple squall for us was a catastrophe for them.

*G*rebes prefer the calm waters of the small craft harbor today rather than the white-capped waves of the open Sound. The diving birds paddle slowly between the piers, diving often, leaving not a ripple on the surface of the water. The grebes avoid the vicinity of loons, which are larger and remain submerged longer. It was the French who named grebes, calling them "sac 'a plomb" (sack of lead) because of their quick dives.

*H*andsome gifts from hermit crabs are numbers of interesting seashells which they  bring to the shoreline. If it were not for the little creatures, many shells would remain unseen in deep water. At water's edge this afternoon are shells, mostly diminutive oyster drills, but some conch shells. One medium-sized horse conch shell is empty, ready to be occupied by yet another hermit crab which has outgrown an earlier shell.

A wounded gull remains with its flock on the beach, although it cannot fly. There is a painful sadness in seeing it so afflicted day after day. William Blake wrote that when a bird is "wounded in the wing, a cherubim does cease to sing." It was he, too, who noted that a bird in a cage "puts all Heaven in a rage." So it is that we watch the disabled laughing gull, finding no joy in its "ha-ha-ha" call.

"Auguries of Innocence;" *The Poetical Works of William Blake;* London: Oxford University Press (1956).

"*Surprised by joy . . . ,*" *is the way Wordsworth put it. And so it is today. The unexpected beauty of a small, wild petunia plant—growing in brambles, flourishing under the most unfavorable conditions—is discovered near the beach, growing in arid sand. The wildflower book records that the flower blooms from May to October but far to the northeast. Yet here it is by the sea, five light purple petals, velvet to the touch!*

"Surprised by Joy" by William Wordsworth.

*Things seen on today's beach walk:
Eleven brown pelicans in a line flying westward. A flock of twenty-eight sanderlings
roosting well up on the beach. Two laughing
gulls mating. Six ruddy turnstones flipping
shells at water's edge. Two upturned horseshoe crabs, one dead, the other very much
alive and, on an offshore post, a cormorant
with its black wings fully extended, drying
after a plunge into the water.*

The approach of summer is felt in the warmth of the south wind today. Early spring flowers have withered, and pelicans have left to nest for a while on the offshore islands.

SPRING WINDS
Winds hurry away,
blowing spring into summer,
sending clouds askew.

The Beach in
Summer

The fullness of June is here! "Now all Nature is alive," wrote the poet George Meredith. Once barren and brown, the dunes brim with life, not only green panic grass but with new plants and wildflowers. Along the line of dunes are small animal tracks, insects, bees and a few butterflies. "Earthworld, airworld, waterworld"— all creation strives for this one season, a time of birth, emergence, and growth.

"The Sweet o' the Year" by George Meredith.
"All in Froth" by Gerard Manley Hopkins. *Summer;* Book Sales, Inc.; Edison, N. J.

The first beach morning glory of the year appears! Its trumpet-like white bloom with a yellow center springs to life in a desolate, sandy area near the fishing pier, an oasis of beauty. Opening before daylight, the bloom will remain until mid-afternoon when it will close its petals, awaiting another sunrise. This trailing plant is a perennial, blooming year after year despite briny floods, freezings and countless mowings.

The sea appears endless today, an expanse of blue water as far as the eye can see. Not a boat is in view, just crystal clear, sparkling water. Byron termed it "the image of eternity." He wrote, ". . . man marks the earth with ruin," but "his control stops with the shore." Today the sea is pristine, untouched by man, just as it was perhaps on the day of creation, just as it was when Iberville first saw it three centuries ago.

"Childe Harold's Pilgrimage" by Lord Byron.

"*The magic hour before sunset,*" the painter Walter Anderson called it, magical because the  world of nature could be grasped and understood better than at other times of day. It is an hour, he wrote, when "*all things are related.*" Like Monet before him, he searched for the right light to illuminate the objects that he painted. Today at the "*magic hour*" we watch as the sun, low in the northwestern sky, emits its warm, slanted rays.

The Horn Island Logs of Walter Inglis Anderson, edited by William S. Sugg, Jr.; Memphis State University Press (1973).

A memory from the distant past, decades ago, comes to mind now for no reason. Often in the 1930s several neighborhood boys swam at Dantzler pier located here. One day five dolphins glided to the pier, playfully joining the boys. Although the frolic lasted only minutes, its memory lingers, very much alive, 70 years later. One of the young lads is still within me, recalling those happy moments so long ago. He is the boy I used to be.

The seashore has a magnetic fascination to mankind, drawing us back to it again and again. Rachel Carson writes that it is "the place of our dim ancestral beginnings." The tidal rhythms, the waves, the wind, the multiple forms of life, she explains, are interesting, but there is a far deeper attraction which springs from the innermost depths of our being. The beach "is a world as old as the earth, a primeval meeting place."

Quoted in *Earth's Echo* by Robert M. Hamma; Sorin Books; Notre Dame, Indiana (2002).

*T*hree little, white cabbage butterflies flit sprightly along the median beside the beach road. Early to appear in spring, they are abhorred by gardeners, because of damage done to planted vegetables and flowers. But one writer prizes the "small whites" (as they are called in Europe) and therefore plants enough for the butterflies and for himself too. Now their pale wings flutter eastward in hasty, low-level flight.

Robert Michael Pyle, author of *Handbook for Butterfly Watchers*; Houghton Mifflin, New York (1992).

There are three striped burrfish on the beach this morning. Floated ashore in the high tide, they lie at water's edge. Part of the puffer fish family, the small creatures are about six inches long. When a predator nears, the burrfish will inflate itself like a balloon. Needle-sharp spines protrude from its body, inhibiting the hungriest predator. Two sharp teeth—one in each jaw—are capable of crushing hard shells.

*Y*ears ago, we listened to the calls of shorebirds and, without much thought, accepted them as merely background sounds of the beach. Lately we hear them differently—as non-verbal language, an exchanging of information. Often the cry of a laughing gull is in a language that we don't comprehend, but sometimes it translates clearly. For example, one gull warns its fellows loudly of our approach, "A man is walking toward our flock."

Attitude influences how things are perceived. Take today's beach walk, for example. Even in the storm's aftermath, there are positive things to observe—the recovery of shorebirds, a pacific sea, the survival of a wildflower. The way we look at things makes a difference. The glass should always be half full, never half empty. There is wisdom in a Chinese adage, "Keep a green branch in your heart and for sure a songbird will come."

Quoted in *Prayer Notes to a Friend* by Edward Hays; Forest of Peace Publishing; Leavenworth, Kansas.

$\mathcal{E}$arly this morning,
a Gulf storm dumped
ten inches of rain on the
beach in a few hours.
High winds and a rising tide pillaged
least tern nests filled with eggs and
fledglings. With a wisdom learned through
the ages by their genus, the birds will mate
again this season. As skies cleared and
winds diminished, the small, white terns
could be seen once again, diving for
minnows, "an affirmation of life," as Albert
Schweitzer put it.

Albert Schweitzer's remarks on receiving the Nobel Prize.

*A*mong the victims of last week's storm is a little sanderling, whose remains lie near the bottom step of the seawall. Washed there, one guesses, in the tempest's surging tide, the bird is but a fluff of white feathers, perhaps an ounce of flesh, now bereft of life. In nature's efficient economy the body will disappear in a few days, nourishing creatures of a lower phylum, its feathers wind-driven, leaving a memory of pleasanter days.

A blue crab, moving deftly in shallow water this morning, is aptly named. Its proper scientific name is *Callinectes sapidus*. The first word means "beautiful swimmer." It shows its grace as it half-swims, half-crawls a few feet from shore. The second word, *sapidus*, means flavorful or savory. Carolus Linnaeus, or whoever named the succulent creature, knew what he was doing. Swimming away now, the crab vanishes into deep water.

*O*n shore is the visible world of shorebirds, seaside plants, insects at water's edge, hermit crabs, barnacles and others. But in the intertidal zone lies a penumbra of unseen domains, countless societies of seaworms, crustaceans, jellyfish, and creatures which look like plants but are actually animals. Others, burrowing deep in the sand, living in convoluted tunnels, are seldom seen by humans. How little is known of their realms!

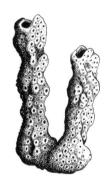

The smell of the sea, a musky fragrance, wafts ashore this afternoon borne on a warm breeze. Not unpleasant to the senses, its pungence is a merging of many things. The decay of organic matter, withered seaweeds, decomposing fish, and moldering plankton—all contribute to the scent. But it is more than those things. It is the aroma of the vast sea itself—the elixir of salt water—a bouquet of new life created in countless forms.

A fish crow perches on a post eating a fledgling mockingbird stolen from a nearby nest. With parental fury, a mockingbird attacks the raptor to no avail. Bestial, you say? Of course, but we forget the untamed wildness of nature. With Blake, we ask, "Did he who made the Lamb, make" the tiger? In the sea, big fish eat small fish. Charles Darwin once reminded a friend of "the horribly cruel works of nature."

"The Tiger" by William Blake.

*S*mall pebbles tumble ashore this morning,
borne by waves, to lie at water's edge among
small shells, bone fragments and jellyfish.
The pebbles are varied shapes, colors and
sizes. Most have very smooth surfaces,
polished during their long trip down the
watercourses from the Appalachian
Mountains. Some are white; others are
brown. Holding one in hand, one
wonders about the beginning of its
journey here perhaps in Cambrian times.

There is a life force—"elan vital," Bergson called it—seen everywhere in nature and shared by man too. A pair of laughing gulls engaged in pre-mating antics today, a leaping mullet, minnows schooling, a hermit crab crawling out of the sea, even shore flies—all possess that spirit of energy which moves living things. Plants, too, produce winged seeds, which have the role of migrating and scattering widely, enhancing the species.

Henri Bergson, French philosopher, (1859-1941).

A mid-summer day's inventory of
the beach: Three gulls fly above the sand
flats looking for detritus. A clutch of peeps,
sanderlings and other sandpipers is at
water's edge pecking for crustaceans.
Nearby two royal terns dive for fish.
Offshore three brown pelicans perch on
posts. A lone fish crow looks seaward.
Quietly, not moving, a great blue heron
stands in the shallows.
By the seawall, a colony
of ants is busily active.

$\mathcal{A}$ large flock of gulls roosts on the beach with no regard for two noisy tractors, roaring by only a few feet away. Accustomed now to encroaching civilization, the birds have no fear of the passing machines. They have adapted to the environment of an urban beach. The accommodation allows for tractors; but when an osprey appears high in the sky, the flock registers alarm, an instinctive response to a wild predator.

The squall approached the mainland from the southwest, making up first over the barrier island. The effect of the driving wind on the sea was dramatic. Foaming white caps under a dark cloud differed from normal waves to the east and west of the squall. Then heavy rain followed the tempest's roiling sea. In a matter of minutes the blow  *had passed, and in its wake is a glassy, calm sea rippled only by jumping mullets.*

HERMIT CRAB

Hermit crab, hauling
your rusty, borrowed seashell,
where are you going?

PELICANS

Five pelicans fly
lazily in summer sky
to a setting sun.

The footprints of the Maker are detected daily on the broad expanse of the beach. In every direction, there He is! The orderly movement of the tides, rising and setting suns and moons, the course of stars, the flight of birds, the passage of fish, atom structures in grains of sand— all are designed by Him. Edna St. Vincent Millay expressed it this way, ". . . God, I can push the grass apart, and lay my finger on Thy heart."

Collected Poems, Edna St. Vincent Millay; Harper Collins, New York (1950).

There is clockwork precision in Nature. Suns and moons rise and set at their appointed hours. Ebbing and flowing, tides move on schedule. Atoms march in exact orbits. Songwriter Bob Dylan wrote that he was in ". . . a perfect, finished plan/like every fallen sparrow/like every grain of sand." And William Cowper expressed it this way: "Nature is but a name for an effect whose cause is God."

"Every Grain of Sand" by Bob Dylan, quoted in *The Strangest Way* by Robert Barron; Orbis Books, New York (2002).
"The Task" by William Cowper (1731-1800).

The towering cumulus clouds moving northward are typical of a summer  *afternoon. Prior to 1800 few people thought much about clouds, which were then called "essences." Billowing now, they are fun to watch, gliding along, changing shapes and densities. Roger Tory Peterson wrote that "clouds are an ever-changing visual feast." And so they are! One after another, they pass overhead, finally disappearing in the north.*

Peterson First Guide to Clouds and Weather by John A. Day and Vincent J. Schaefer; Houghton Mifflin, New York (1991).

*T*he warm, summer water flooding ashore at high tide brings with it many comb jellyfish, very fragile little ctenophores. When disturbed at night, they emit a glow, a bioluminescence. In a poem, John Hay writes that the jelly is nine-tenths water, "a pulsing flower" of the sea, possessing "delicate, diaphanous engineering with magic in its appetite." Today the comb, eight pinkish rays, shimmers and sparkles with color in the sunlight.

The Way to the Salt Marsh by John Hay; University Press of New England, Hanover and London (1998).

A half dozen butterflies are visiting a sand dune at noon, stopping briefly at its small wildflower blooms. Monarchs like hot, bright days like today. But their activity differs. Four flit fitfully from flower to flower, energetic in collecting nectar. The other two, resting calmly on plants, unmoving, wings outstretched, enjoy the warmth of the sunshine. Then the busy four fly to the next dune, leaving the sunbathers behind.

*A*t midday there are about a dozen
shrimp boats offshore, all at anchor, bows
pointed up into the wind, like so many gulls.
Two of the crafts are rafted together, port to
starboard side, their crews
probably asleep below
deck. Many shrimpers
do their arduous work
at night when it is
cooler, resting during
the heat of the day.
It is said too that
large shoals of shrimp
are found more easily
at night, gleaming in the dark sea.

Close your eyes for a moment; relax; take three deep breaths. Imagine that you are sitting on the seawall as the sun sets. There are no sounds except from shorebirds feeding quietly at water's edge. Feel the soft, scented sea breeze against your face. White caps break on the shore. The cares and worries of the day recede. You are alone and at peace. You bask in the warmth of the day. There! You have enjoyed a one-minute holiday!

*T*wo yellow-crowned night herons are summer residents in the swamp grass west of the fishing pier. Through most of the day they rest quietly, as if frozen. After sunset the birds walk slowly in shallow water, preferring small tidal pools left by the ebbing tide. There one stands motionless, then with a quick darting of its head, a small crab is captured. One supposes that the feeding will continue through the night until sunrise.

A friend calls the beach a cathedral. And so it is. Is there a more blessed place than where sea and land meet? One is reminded of Jacob, awaking from a dream, saying, "Surely the Lord is in this place, and I knew it not!—This is the gate of heaven." But this hallowed beach has no priority as God's abode. He is also near hospital beds, laughing children, dining tables, offices, the bereaved, and among other places.

Genesis 28:16-17.

There are not many fiddler crabs on our beach, but there are a few. Once aquatic, the little creatures have chosen to live on land, away from the sea which was their home. They have a sandy color which camouflages them nicely in their habitat. Crab tracks in the sand near the dunes are more often seen than the fiddlers themselves. Yet they sometimes appear, the males holding one large claw as if it were a weapon or a fiddle.

At high tide five skiffs are anchored near the small craft harbor channel, the fishermen casting shrimp-baited rigs for speckled trout. High tide is prime time for speckles. Once Saint Francis, sitting in

a skiff, was given a nice carp. He accepted it joyfully, calling it "Brother Fish," but returned it to the water. There the carp remained, playing by his boat until Francis, having ended a prayer, instructed it to swim away.

Through the Year with Francis of Assisi, edited by Murray Bodo; St. Anthony Messenger Press, Cincinnati, Ohio (1993).

Thoreau once said that a beach is a graveyard. And to a degree it is true. Here we find dead birds, fish, jellies and other creatures washed ashore. But there is also life. For instance, the lifeless vine, planted last month on the dune, now sprouts a leaf. It is as Job said, there is always hope for a dead tree. Life renews itself. An empty, whelk egg case lying at water's edge today holds promise of a new generation of marine snails.

Henry David Thoreau (1817-1862).
Job 14:7.

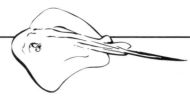

*J*uly and August are months in which
stingrays lie only inches offshore. Today
in crystal clear water, three rays are here.
Heads facing the beach, they are motionless,
their long whip-like tails extended. Then,
sensing danger, they swim away as if birds
on graceful wings. If evolutionists are right,
sea creatures will become land ones. Perhaps
in future eons rays may fly in the air, as
they now "fly" through the water.

Fish and shorebirds (and perhaps other creatures too) are fearful of shadows. To them a shadow means instant danger, probably an instinctive dread of raptors. Today the shade of an overhead cloud falls on a school of minnows swimming near the beach. In their alarm the little fish do not disperse, as one might expect, but bunch together in a tight pattern for protection. For them the shadow means the perilous approach of a large fish.

$\mathcal{F}$ollowing an early morning squall with heavy rainfall and gusty winds, a breathless calm has spread over the sea. Gone are the thick, dark, rain clouds. Goethe wrote of similar quietness, "Like a mirror sleeps the ocean . . . not a breath of wind is stirring . . . not the lifting of a wave." The sea's glassy surface extends far to the south, undisturbed by jumping mullet, diving terns, or even by passing dolphins.

"A Calm at Sea" by Johann Wolfgang von Goethe; *Poems of the Sea,* edited by J. B. McClatchy: Alfred A. Knopf, New York (2001).

So often blue and peaceful, the sea today is slate-colored, reflecting dark clouds overhead. It is a mystic, "sunless sea," as Coleridge described it. From the beginning of time, man has pondered its depths and mysteries. Our word, "soul," Edward Hays says, comes from an old Germanic noun, "saiwalo," meaning "from the sea." There was once a Teutonic myth that people's souls originated in and finally returned to the sea.

Prayer Notes to a Friend by Edward Hays; Forest of Peace Publishing; Leavenworth, Kansas (2002).

The task of finding food is a daily challenge for shorebirds. Every day at first light the hunt for sustenance begins. For gulls it means scouring the shoreline for detritus washed ashore during the night. For sanderlings the chore is to peck into wet sand for little crustaceans and crab eggs. For terns the burden is to dive into the sea for fish. Unlike nut-saving squirrels, birds know hunger as a constant, daily visitor.

The great blue heron which is a frequent visitor to the beach may have a personality defect. He doesn't tolerate people very well. Some beach walkers have nicknamed him, "Grumpy." A loner, the long-legged heron, may stand for hours in shallow water awaiting a small fish to swim near. Then with a lightning-quick movement of its head, the bird grabs a fish in its bill, gracefully flying away to a less populated part of the beach.

*H*eavy rain has dropped several inches of fresh water onto the beach, resulting in scars in the sand from the seawall to the shoreline. Some ten feet wide, the watercourses show where rainwater had drained southward into the sea. The rains also revealed a few interesting long-buried shells, as sand which had covered them was washed seaward. Although the rain has stopped, sodden shorebirds still roost in flocks by the seawall.

*Y*esterday a grassy area near the fishing pier was graced by a number of beach morning glories, beautiful white blooms with delicate yellow centers. Wildflowers, they grow in dry sand, blooming from mid-summer to October. Victims of mowing machines, they are now gone, but will soon blossom again. As Horace observed in the First Century B.C., "You can drive out Nature with a pitchfork, but she always comes hurrying back."

*T*hese are days
in late summer when
hermit crabs crawl out
of the sea onto the beach to bask in warm
sunshine. A dozen or so lie there today,
their shells' apertures facing the sky. When
there is no activity, the creatures partially
leave the shells, enjoying the pleasant day.
Now they are very vulnerable to shorebirds,
so at the slightest disturbance, the crabs
withdraw deep into their shells with only
claws visible.

Tomorrows become yesterdays in the swift passage of time. And all the least terns, except one lone bird, have departed the beach. Flocks of our smallest tern now wing their way southward, migrating perhaps to some rocky Brazilian shore. Although there may be others left behind too, only one remains here. It flies over a calm sea, head-down, searching for small fish, its long, narrow wings beating more rapidly than those of other terns.

The frail fragments of a bird egg are found in an empty nest on the sand beach. The stark nest, merely a depression in the sand, a few dry twigs, once was home to a pair of least terns. The egg may have spawned a healthy chick—one now flying south in a migrating flock. That crucible of life in most of its forms, an egg is the beginning of existence on earth, a holy cup, a cornucopia brimming with expectancy and vivacity.

West of the Chandeleur Islands there are
many acres of underwater meadows where
green fields of lush grass grow only a few feet
below the surface. When the
water is clear, the
tall blades are
seen bending
gracefully
in the sea
currents, as if wafted by wind. This is the
season when nature harvests grass, sending
it floating ashore. On the beach are large
amounts of the grass, once green, now
brown, drying in the summer sun.

A pod of dolphins swims offshore near the deep water markers, four or five of them, diving, sometimes leaping far out of the water. They are our cousins, you see, warm-blooded mammals with brains larger than those of humans. Dolphins communicate, too, uttering sounds, conversing with others in the pod. Their affability is expressed in many ways, such as by swimming alongside small boats or looking inquiringly at fellow swimmers.

$\mathcal{P}$retty little coquina shells, only an inch in size, tumble in the waves today. Once bivalves, the dead shells are separated, the clams which occupied them long gone. However, live coquinas are near at hand, burying themselves in shallow water. Both upper and lower valves, almost identical, have delicate colors—yellows and pinks— varying from shell to shell. Often called butterfly shells, coquinas resemble small butterfly wings.

$\mathcal{B}$right, warm sunshine is a requirement for most butterflies, as one notes today. Several sulphur butterflies had been visiting flowers on the sand dune. When a cloud obscured the sun, the butterflies stopped feeding and remained, wings uplifted, on branches of bushes. A few minutes later, after the cloud had passed, they began flying once again. Hot, bright, sunshiny days are the very best ones for butterfly watching.

*W*hat fine companions on an early beach walk—morning glories and two alfalfa butterflies! The yellow "winged flowers," as they are called, visit each morning glory bloom, feeding briefly at the innermost ovaries which contain seeds. The little butterflies don't harm the plants, but may carry pollen which helps produce future growth. After a while, they fly away, leaving the morning glories to bask in the warm sunlight.

*S*omeone had walked this beach earlier in the day, because there is evidence of his or her presence. Near water's edge six oyster shells have been neatly and precisely placed all in a line. It calls to mind Lewis Carroll's little ditty, ". . . and all the little Oysters stood and waited in a row." And what of the person who arranged the shells so nicely?

Did he or she expect them to be found, to become a source of wonder?

*C*elebrate the act of "being."
At this very hour standing on
the shoreline, looking
seaward, feeling and
smelling a musky wind,
sensing the sun's
warmth on face and
arms, hearing the cries
of shorebirds—it is the
reality of experience. At this time, we are
the center of all creation, absorbing the
essence of this single episode of the day. It
is a "sacrament of the moment," a cherished
gift to be fully grasped and enjoyed now.

There is a woman who reads these paragraphs daily, but is disabled and cannot leave her chair. Vicariously, she walks the

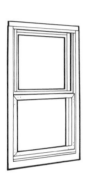

beach, mentally experiencing the joys of God's wonderful world. She has found that her window, too, is a blessing. Looking out, she sees trees, birds, squirrels and clouds during the day, and stars at night—nature framed for her viewing. How few of us take time to see the world right outside our windows!